Vision Impact!

*An Interactive Workbook to Help You Write Your Vision,
Implement Your Plan and Impact Your World*

Bernard K. Haynes

Vision Impact! Workbook - *An Interactive Workbook to Help You Write Your Vision, Implement Your Plan and Impact Your World*

by Bernard K. Haynes
Copyright © 2017 Lead to Impact™, LLC

For more materials and information contact:

Bernard K. Haynes
Lead to Impact, LLC
bhaynes@leadtoimpact.com
www.leadtoimpact.com

ISBN # 978-0-9961945-6-3
For Worldwide Distribution
Printed in the U.S.A

Edited by: Shannon Rasmussen

Published by:
Lead to Impact LLC
3740 Falls Trail
Winston, GA 30187

Table of Contents

Introduction

"No individual has any right to come into the world and go out of it without leaving behind him distinct and legitimate reasons for having passed through it." George Washington Carver

The purpose of the Vision Impact! Interactive Workbook is to encourage, equip and empower you to create a written vision plan for the future God purposed for your life. Many people attempt to live their lives without a real plan. Imagine a football coach trying to lead a football team without a game plan, a builder trying to build a house without a blueprint, a pastor trying to lead a church without a vision from God.

All of the examples above perpetuate confusion because the leaders are trying to operate without a plan. You do the same thing when you attempt to live your life without a clear plan. Without a clear vision you can end up going around in circles, living an unproductive and unsatisfied life.

I am not promising a magical formula: a guarantee if you read this material and answer each question in detail that your vision will come to pass without any struggles. Nor am I promising that if you follow the instructions within this manual, your vision will happen in thirty days. Just know that to walk in your vision you must make sacrifices, overcome challenges, face opposition and work your plan. If you apply the practical instruction, insight and inspiration found within this workbook, it will help you move in the direction God destined for you.

The fact that you are alive right now, the fact that you have gone through everything you have gone through and the fact that the enemy could not take you out is evidence that God has a greater vision for your life. You are going to have to fight through everything and everyone who is trying to keep you from realizing and living out your vision.

The enemy is trying his best to keep you in the dark about your true vision. He wants you to give up because of the pain of your past. He wants you to walk away from your promise because of the problems in your current situation. He wants you to live life discouraged and defeated instead of encouraged and empowered. Today is your day to realize your vision, write your plan and take action.

Chapter 1

Vision Impact

Habakkuk 1-3

Vision Impact!

"Where there is no vision the people perish." Proverbs 29:18

It was the vision of equal rights for all people that inspired Dr. Martin Luther King, Jr. to crusade for civil rights. It was the vision of a new nation of people that led Abraham to leave his homeland to follow God to an unfamiliar land. It was the vision of greater discovery that motivated George Washington Carver to discover over 300 different uses for the peanut. It was the vision of becoming a fisher of men that led Peter to leave his fishing business to follow Jesus. Vision demands change.

What is possibly more satisfying than knowing the God of the universe designed you with a unique vision to impact the world? His vision for you is

> *"Visions are birthed in the heart and mind of an individual who is frustrated and tired of the way things are in contrast to the way they believe things could and should be."*

not a one-size-fits-all, but it is uniquely fashioned to fit you. No matter who you are, what country or continent you live on or what side of the tracks you are from, God created you with a unique vision that no one in this world can live but you.

Regardless of where you are in life, (your age, financial status, educational level or family background) your unique vision positions you to impact your home, community, city, state, nation and ultimately the world! The desire to impact those connected to your vision empowers you to move past the failures of yesterday, the excuses of today and the fears of tomorrow.

When you take the initiative to activate your vision, it will:

- Give you the correct directions and coordinates to follow.
- Let you know where you currently are and what turns you need to make to get to your destination.
- Provide the inspiration and motivation you need when it seems everything and everyone is against you.
- Expand your thinking, increase your sight and elevate your walk.

Get ready to take hold of your vision and impact your world!

Personal Application Questions:

1.   Why do you believe it is important for you to have a clear vision from God?

_____

_____

_____

_____

_____

2.   What do you need to do to intentionally seek God's vision for your life?

_____

_____

_____

_____

_____

3.   What are you truly passionate about? Describe in detail.

_____

_____

_____

_____

_____

4. If you had to stand face to face with God right now can you honestly say to Him that you are living the life He designed for you? If not, what do you need to do? If yes, what do you need to do to stay on track?

_____

_____

_____

_____

_____

5. What changes from living your vision would you want to have brought into your family and community that would be remembered for generations?

_____

_____

_____

_____

_____

6.   Read Genesis 12: 1-3. In this chapter God gave Abraham an incredible vision that in order for him to live he had to totally trust God. What did God ask him to do? If God asked you to leave everything that you are comfortable and familiar with to go to a place with no point of reference, could you totally trust Him to make the move? What would it take for you to trust God at this level?

_____

_____

_____

_____

_____

_____

_____

_____

_____

_____

_____

_____

_____

_____

_____

"There is no passion to be found playing small – in settling for a life that is less than the one you are capable of living.   Nelson Mandela

Get off Your I-285

"The Lord our God spoke to us at Horeb saying, you have stayed long enough at this mountain. Turn and take your journey…"   Deuteronomy 1:6-7

Several years ago, my wife and I were traveling on I-285 in Atlanta going to a shopping center. To those who may not know, I-285 is the by-pass loop that goes around the perimeter of Atlanta. What should have been a forty-five minute trip took us an hour and a half.

I will never forget riding around I-285. I said to my wife, "I believe we have passed the airport twice." She looked at me with frustration in her eyes, and said with anger in her voice, "No, this

> *"Now is the time for you to reach the destination you've been searching for. It is time to end the insanity. It is time to change direction and get new results. It is time to enjoy what's inside the perimeter of your life."*

is our third time." I knew then it was time to ask for proper directions. I let go of my I-know-where–I-am-going ego and asked for directions. It didn't make sense to continue riding around in circles when help was a phone call away.

I believe to this day one of two things occurred: I received bad directions or I didn't write the directions down correctly. My wife says that I did not listen. In any case, we wasted valuable time and gas riding around the perimeter of Atlanta.

The children of Israel experienced the first I-285 experience. It took forty years for them to complete a less than two-week journey. They spent forty years wandering in circles instead of enjoying the prosperous land God promised them. They exhausted valuable time and energy going around and around the same mountain, passing through the same desert land because they refused to obey God's directions.

The children of Israel forfeited forty years of abundant living in the land flowing with milk and honey because they allowed fear, rebellion and disobedience to block their promise. It wasn't the distance to the land that stood in their way of receiving the promise; it was the attitude of their hearts.

8

The children of Israel forfeited forty years of abundant living in the land flowing with milk and honey because they allowed fear, rebellion and disobedience to block their promise. It wasn't the distance to the land that stood in their way of receiving the promise; it was the attitude of their hearts.

Spend some quality time in prayer listening to God for His guidance. You may have to do things totally different from what you have been doing or you may have to make some small changes that will bring great results. Whatever He is telling you to do differently, do it and watch the results. Answer the following questions in detail on what God is telling you to do differently in your:

1. Relationship with Him:

_____

_____

_____

_____

_____

2. Relationship with your spouse or finance:

_____

_____

_____

_____

_____

3. Relationship with your children:

_____

_____

_____

_____

_____

4. Relationship with your family and friends:

_____

_____

_____

_____

_____

5. Finances:

_____

_____

_____

_____

_____

6. Physical health:

_____

_____

_____

_____

_____

7. Work, Career or School:

_____

_____

_____

_____

_____

8. Thought life:

_____

_____

_____

_____

_____

9. Social life:

_____

_____

_____

_____

_____

"We are what we repeatedly do. Excellence, therefore, is not an act but a habit." Aristotle

7 Keys to Unlock the Power of Your Vision

"I will stand upon my watch, and set me upon the tower and will watch to see what he will say unto me and what I shall answer when I am reproved." Habakkuk 2:1

Habakkuk 2:2 is an often-quoted scripture for ministries and churches that desire to move forward with a corporate vision. Yearlong vision campaigns are developed and implemented in conjunction with this verse. Conferences and seminars are created with this verse as the main theme.

I have seen people get excited when they hear this verse proclaimed by a pastor or teacher. They shout, high-five their neighbors and dance around the sanctuary

> **What is Vision?**
>
> *Vision is a clear mental picture of a preferable future God communicates to an individual. The individual becomes so committed to the vision that he or she will pursue after it despite any obstacles or challenges.*
>
> *Vision is seeing farther than you can see with your physical eyes.*

with great enthusiasm upon the declaration of this word. There have been songs and books written about Habakkuk 2:2. Needless to say, this is a very popular verse when it comes to talking about writing a vision.

It is sad to report that, after hearing this powerful verse proclaimed, many people still have not made the effort or taken the time to write a personal and/or family vision.

It sounds inspiring and motivating to hear a teacher or preacher proclaiming, "Write the vision and make it plain." I have discovered, however, that it takes more than an inspirational message or weekend seminar about vision to make things happen. It takes a concentrated effort to write your vision and an unwavering commitment to implement it.

You must determine to not let the fear of failure, fear of rejection, excuses, others' opinions and procrastination hinder you any longer. You must make up your mind to pursue your vision even if you have to do it afraid. If you begin to make the effort to move your vision forward, God will send the necessary resources and people you need to make things happen.

Now is the time to unlock the power of your vision. After spending quality time studying and meditating on Habakkuk 2:1-4, I extrapolated seven keys to unlocking the power of your vision. If you implement these seven keys, your vision will have a powerful impact on your family, friends, community, city, country and, ultimately, the world.

Answer the following questions to help you unlock the power of your vision.

1. Vision is revealed to the person in position to listen.

a. What do you need to do to get in position to hear God's direction?

_____

_____

_____

_____

_____

_____

b. What things or people do you need to eliminate from your life to hear His directions?

_____

_____

_____

_____

_____

_____

2. Vision must be written down.

a. Why would God tell you to write out your vision?

_____

_____

_____

_____

_____

b. Why is it important for you to write your vision?

_____

_____

_____

_____

_____

3. Vision must be made plain.

a. Why do you need to make your vision plain?

_____

_____

_____

_____

_____

b. What will happen if your vision is not plain?

_____

_____

_____

_____

_____

4. Vision must be posted.

a. Why do you believe it is important to post your vision?

_____

_____

_____

_____

_____

b. Where can you post your vision to keep you and others on track?

_____

_____

_____

_____

_____

5. Vision overcomes obstacles.

a. What obstacles are present in your life that you have allowed to hinder your vision?

_____

_____

_____

_____

_____

b. How can you overcome these obstacles to living your vision?

_____

_____

_____

_____

_____

6. Vision will manifest itself in God's time.

a. Why would God require you to wait on the vision?

_____

_____

_____

_____

_____

b. Why is waiting sometimes difficult? How can you go through your waiting period with confidence that God will see you through?

_____

_____

_____

_____

_____

7. Vision must be lived by faith.

a. How can you live your vision by faith when your circumstances paint a different picture?

_____

_____

_____

_____

_____

b. Why does God require you to work on your vision and not sit like you are waiting at a bus stop?

_____

_____

_____

_____

_____

"Hold fast to dreams for if dreams die, life is a broken winged bird that cannot fly."
Langston Hughes

Vision Challenged

"For forty days the Philistines came forward every morning and evening and took his stand"
I Samuel 17:26

Have you ever been challenged by a situation that made you want to quit? Have you ever had to face a challenge that made you feel incapable and insufficient?

Israel was confronted by Goliath, an impressive and seemingly unconquerable ten-foot giant (I Samuel 17:8-9). He spent forty days calling out King Saul and the Army of Israel, telling them they did not stand a chance against him. He overwhelmed them with such fear that, whenever he came out to challenge them, they ran and hid.

Goliath's intense challenge had King Saul, the one person who was able to stand against him, hiding in fear. Every morning and every evening for forty days,

> *"The person who really wants to do something finds a way; the other person finds an excuse."*

Goliath presented his challenge to the Army of Israel. For forty days, they lived in fear intimidated by the giant. For forty days, Goliath flaunted his size and strength, daring Saul to send someone to fight him.

This is how the giants in your life will challenge your vision. Your giants will come at you morning, noon and evening, day after day, relentlessly trying to derail you. Their intentions are to steal, kill and literally destroy the vision that lives within you.

God desires to use your pressure situations to shape you like a priceless diamond. Earthly diamonds are formed when enough pressure is produced ninety miles under the earth's surface, along with temperatures of 2,200 degrees Fahrenheit. The experts say that without these particular conditions, diamonds cannot be formed.

Without intense pressures in your life, you cannot become all God destined you to be. He allows pressure situations in your life for you to see His strength and your weakness, His wisdom and your foolishness, His ability and your inability and His infiniteness and your finiteness.

Do not run from your challenges. God knows what you are dealing with. He knows your marriage is struggling; your finances are no longer funny, but hilarious. He knows your health is not good, your children are out of control and your job is downsizing. He knows all of your situations. Can I tell you what else He knows? He knows who He created you to become.

Personal Application Questions:

1. Why do you believe the enemy's attack against you living your vision is so intense?

_____

_____

_____

_____

_____

_____

2. How can you overcome the attacks of the enemy who is trying to steal, kill and destroy your vision?

_____

_____

_____

_____

_____

_____

3. List at least three challenges that you are dealing with in your life right now?

_____

_____

_____

_____

_____

_____

4. How can you gain victory over each of the challenges you listed?

_____
_____
_____
_____
_____
_____
_____

5. Whate is the promise that Christ gives you in John 10:10? Why can you trust Him for this promise?

_____
_____
_____
_____
_____
_____
_____

6. In your own words what does it mean for you to live the more abundant life?

_____
_____
_____
_____
_____
_____
_____

"Though no one can go back and make a brand new start, anyone can start from now and make a brand new ending." Sir Winston Churchill

Excuses are Not Accepted. Get the Job Done

"The sick man answered Him, "Sir, I have no man to put me into the pool when the water is stirred up, but while I am coming another steps down before me." John 5:7

What excuses have you allowed to keep you from living your vision? Have you told yourself that you are not smart enough to get the promotion, you do not deserve to live a better life, you are not articulate enough to teach, or you will never make enough money to live debt free? Have you convinced yourself with your excuses that your vision is impossible for you or out of your reach?

The man at the pool of Bethesda had waited at the pool for thirty-eight long years to receive his healing. Every time he went to the pool for healing after the angel stirred the water, someone beat him to the punch. His situation looked impossible.

Excuses people make for not living their vision:

- **I don't believe God can use me.**
- **I don't have enough time.**
- **I don't have enough money.**
- **I didn't have my father in my life.**
- **I don't have the right education or experience.**
- **I am too old or too young.**
- **I didn't come from the right background.**

Making excuses infected this man's life so greatly he could not see his healer standing in front of him. When Jesus asked him if he wanted to be made whole, the first words that came out of his mouth were excuses as to why he could not get to the water to receive his healing.

He told Jesus, "Sir, I have no man to put me into the pool when the water is stirred up, but while I am coming, another steps down before me" (Luke 5:7). Jesus did not ask him what or who was keeping him from entering the pool. He wanted to know if the man desired to be made whole. The man's excuses could have cost him his healing.

You do not know what you can accomplish until you do it. It doesn't matter if it hasn't been done before; do it anyway. It doesn't matter if no one will go with you; go by yourself. It doesn't matter if you don't get encouragement from your family or friends; encourage yourself.

If God asks you the question, "Do you want to be made whole?" jump up, tell Him yes, and then do exactly what He tells you without any excuses. When you decide to stop making excuses, you can possess your promises and live out your destiny.

Answer the following questions to help you overcome your excuses.

1. What excuses have you made that have held you hostage from living your vision? List your excuses.

_____

_____

_____

_____

_____

_____

_____

_____

2. What steps do you need to take to overcome each excuse you listed?

_____

_____

_____

_____

_____

_____

_____

_____

3. Why do you continue to make excuses when God has shown you what to do?

_____
_____
_____
_____
_____
_____
_____
_____
_____

4. Read Genesis 3 & 4. List 2 excuses Moses made when God gave him His vision. What did God do to encourage Moses after each excuse? How would have you responded to God, if He had presented you with a vision of this magnitude? Please be honest with yourself.

_____
_____
_____
_____
_____
_____
_____
_____
_____
_____
_____
_____
_____

5. Reflection: What one significant thing could you accomplish in your life in the next 12 months if you stopped making excuses and just do it? How would accomplishing this significant thing make your life and/or family better?

_____

_____

_____

_____

_____

_____

_____

_____

_____

_____

_____

_____

_____

"No individual has any right to come into the world and go out of it without leaving behind him distinct and legitimate reasons for having passed through it." George Washington Carver

Chapter 2
Know Your Purpose
Jeremiah 1

Know Your Purpose

"Before I formed you in the womb I knew you, and before you were born I consecrated you; I have appointed you a prophet to the nations." Jeremiah 1:5

Are you clear about your life's overarching purpose? God did not meticulously design you to live a haphazard life full of frustration and confusion. He created you with a unique purpose to pursue. Without purpose, you will never experience the level of fulfillment that is possible for your life.

Purpose is your unique life assignment designed by God. It provides the direction for your daily living. It provides the foundation for your values, vision and goals. It gives meaning to everything you do in your personal, family, social and professional life.

Purpose is bigger than your job, career or what you do. It is a calling. It is a mission. It is an overall theme for your life that transcends your daily activities.

Your life purpose is unique to you. No one else in the world can fulfill your purpose, but you. Whether it concerns an area explored by many or by only a few, what matters is no one can approach it the way you can.

If you have not experienced the level of success you know you are capable of or if you have felt as if something is missing from your life, take note of this very important principle:

> **You are not defined:**
> - *By who others say you are.*
> - *By your job, title, position or possessions.*
> - *By your past failures or mistakes.*

You will only experience true success in your life to the extent you are clear about your life's purpose.

God created you with the desire to pursue your purpose. Without it, you are paralyzed by stagnation, crippled by fear, bored by the daily routine or frustrated by failure. Our inherent need for purpose gives rise to questions such as, "Who am I?" "Why am I here?" or "What is the point to life?"

As God begins to reveal the answers to these questions, you will learn that your purpose will not just magically happen. It will not progress forward without your full participation. You must pursue it with a tireless, dedicated work ethic. You are responsible for the intentional fulfillment of your purpose so the world may benefit from your contributions.

When you realize your life's purpose, everything changes. Your desires, the way you approach life, the people you associate with, the material you read and the things you listen to will change to help bring your purpose into proper focus.

When your deepest needs are met, you feel encouraged and empowered. This focus gives rise to greater clarity about who you are, what you stand for and where you are going. A sense of inspired action will naturally rise up inside of you when you are living passionately with clear direction and a purpose to live for.

Answering the following questions about your purpose will help you become the person God destined you to be. Remember this is about who you are and not what you do. Please take some quality time seeking God for your life's overarching purpose. Allow Him to speak to you in an intimate way as you pray, read and meditate on His Word.

Personal application questions to help you realize your purpose:

1. What are your unique gifts and abilities that God has given you?

_____

_____

_____

_____

_____

_____

_____

2. What are your deepest desires within you?

_____

_____

_____

_____

_____

_____

_____

3. What experiences in life were really fulfilling to you?

_____

_____

_____

_____

_____

_____

_____

4. What do you do that causes you to forget what time it is because it brings you great joy and satisfaction?

_____

_____

_____

_____

_____

_____

_____

5. What would you do with your life if you had all the money you needed?

_____

_____

_____

_____

_____

_____

_____

6. What are your non-negotiable core values?

_____

_____

_____

_____

_____

_____

7. What are some challenges, difficulties and hardships you have overcome or are in the process of overcoming? How did you overcome them, or how are you overcoming them?

_____

_____

_____

_____

_____

_____

_____

8. What legacy do you want to leave for future generations?

_____

_____

_____

_____

_____

_____

_____

Once your purpose becomes clearer, you need to create a purpose statement. Your purpose statement is who you believe God has created you to be. From your answers to the eight purpose questions, write down your purpose statement and begin to live it.

My Purpose Statement:

_____

_____

_____

_____

_____

_____

_____

_____

_____

_____

_____

_____

_____

Once you realize your overarching purpose it is the single most transforming event in your life and all else flows from it. Bernard Haynes

In Position for Purpose

"And they took him and threw him into the pit. Now the pit was empty, without any water in it."
Genesis 37:24

A couple of years ago, I became curious about what it took for a professional basketball team to become a repeat champion. I researched professional basketball champions over the last thirty years to find out what characteristics make repeat champions.

I discovered from my research teams that won multiple championships possessed players and coaches who understood their position on the team. Each player knew what his main responsibility and role was in making his or her team champions. They made a commitment as a unified team that everyone would play his position at a high level every game.

> *"The ultimate measure of a man is not where he stands in moments of comfort and convenience, but where he stands at times of challenge and controversy." Dr. Martin Luther King, Jr*

They decided to put the team above the individual. This required each player to give up his personal success for the team. This kind of dedication and commitment took a major adjustment in their thinking. For some players, it took a transformation in how they approached and played each game. The players from repeat championship teams understood that when the team wins, everyone wins.

I learned from my study of these multiple championship teams that there are seven key positions (point guard, shooting guard, power forward, small forward, center, sixth man and coach) that must be performed in every game with excellence.

Joseph was an excellent example of an individual who understood his purpose, even in the midst of very difficult situations. The dream God gave him (in Genesis 37) of ruling over his brothers and father caused him a great deal of turmoil, beginning when his brothers threw him in a pit. But he did not allow any of the turmoil he encountered to dissuade him from living his purpose. When he was thrown into the pit, he kept looking up.

As a slave in Potiphar's house, Joseph's character remained strong, and positioned him for greatness. When Potiphar's wife made repeated sexual advances toward him, he remained committed to his purpose. When he was thrown in prison, he consistently lived his purpose and found favor with the warden, guards and inmates. When the butler forgot him and he remained in prison for two more years, his confidence in his purpose did not fail.

When Joseph stood before Pharaoh to interpret his dream, he stood boldly and communicated the purpose for Pharaoh's dreams. His courage to interpret the king's dream without fear opened the door for his promotion to Prime Minister of Egypt. Throughout Joseph's life, he displayed a concentrated effort that kept him in tune to God's purpose in spite of his current situations.

After studying the key positions on repeat basketball championship teams and the life of Joseph, I realized seven key positions of purpose for life. I know that there are more positions to your purpose, but I believe after intense prayer and study that these seven are vitally important in fulfilling your God given purpose. Notice I said God

Seven Positions of Purpose
An analogy of key positions on a basketball team.

Coach – Communicate
Point Guard – Concentration
Shooting Guard – Consistency
Small Forward – Confidence
Power Forward – Courage
Center – Character
6th Man - Commitment

given purpose and not man or self-given. I believe if these seven positions of purpose are applied in your daily life then you will see your purpose prosper and your life improve.

Spend some serious quality time in prayer and meditation to answer the following questions about what you need to do to get in and stay in your position for purpose. These seven positions are not an exhaustive list, but I believe they are key to living your purpose with power. **Read Genesis chapters 37, 39-41 to see how Joseph's life exemplified the seven positions of purpose.**

1. Character

"So he left everything he owned in Joseph's charge; and with him there he did not concern himself with anything except the food which he ate." Genesis 39:6

> *Your Character is who you are when no one is looking and what you are willing to stand for when everyone is looking.*

    A. Character is displayed in the actions of a person under pressure.

    B. Your character is revealed by your actions and not the words you speak.

    C. Godly character in an individual communicates credibility and respect and earns trust.

1. What three character traits do you value the most? Why do you value these traits?

_____

_____

_____

_____

_____

2. What three key character traits do you need to develop or work on? What steps are you taking to develop these character traits?

_____

_____

_____

_____

_____

3. What character strengths have you gained from a negative experience?

_____

_____

_____

_____

4. Reflecting on your life, tell about a time where you had to show Godly character in a situation when it would have been easier (so you think) to do the wrong thing?

_____

_____

_____

_____

_____

"Be more concerned about your character than your reputation. Your character is what you really are, while your reputation is merely what others think you are." Dale Carnegie

2. Commitment

"It came about after these events that his master's wife looked with desire at Joseph, and she said, lie with me. But he refused and said to his master's wife, Behold with me here, my master does not concern himself with anything in the house and he has put all that he owns in my charge. There is no one greater in this house than I, and he has withheld nothing from me except you, because you are his wife. How then could I do this great evil and sin against God." Genesis 39: 7-9

Commitment is a binding agreement between the heart, mind and emotions that moves an individual on a course of action to pursue his purpose.

    A. Commitment originates in the heart.

    B. Commitment is demonstrated by action.

    C. Commitment opens the door for opportunities.

1. In what ways has a lack of commitment kept you from living your purpose?

_____

_____

_____

_____

_____

2. What are the hardest commitments you have struggled to keep while working towards your purpose? What do you need to do to remain committed to your purpose even when intense struggles are present?

_____

_____

_____

_____

_____

3. What are you willing to sacrifice or give up in order to live your purpose with power?

_____

_____

_____

_____

_____

4. Reflection: Discuss a time in your Christian walk that you made a promise to commit to something, but after a short time your commitment fizzled away. What would you do differently?

_____

_____

_____

_____

_____

There's a difference between interest and commitment. When you're interested in doing something, you do it only when circumstance permit. When you're committed to something, you accept no excuses, only results." Unknown

3. Concentrate

"As she spoke to Joseph day after day, he did not listen to her to lie beside her or be with her."
Genesis 39:10

Concentrate is to direct your thoughts, attention and actions toward your desired purpose.

A. A concentrated purpose frees you to embrace your vision to produce powerful and lasting results.

B. Do not neglect your focus by trying to do or be everything. There can be a danger in focusing on too many pursuits.

- You become exhausted and burned out.

- You experiment with different goals and never achieve real satisfaction.

- You procrastinate because too many projects compete for your time.

- You become distracted from your ultimate goals

1. What one or two strengths in your life do you need to concentrate on more?

_____

_____

_____

_____

_____

_____

2. Name at least two distractions in your life that have kept you from focusing on your purpose.

_____

_____

_____

_____

_____

_____

3. How can you maintain focus on your purpose despite the distractions you listed?

_____

_____

_____

_____

_____

4. Reflecting on your life – How has a lack of focus kept you from living your purpose? How can focus help you live your purpose?

_____

_____

_____

_____

_____

"Many of life's failures are people who did not realize how close they were to success when they gave up." Thomas Edison

4. Consistency

"So Joseph found favor in his sight and became his personal servant…" Genesis 39: 4

"The chief jailer committed to Joseph's charge all the prisoners who were in the jail…" V. 22

"You shall be over my house and according to your command all my people shall do homage; only in the throne I will be greater than you." Genesis 41: 40

Consistency is a reliable, dependable and coherent approach to daily living that aligns you with your purpose. This daily approach is not a system of habits, but a progressive attitude in moving forward in your purpose even when adjustments and changes have to be made.

    A. Consistent living empowers you to overcome the distractions and temptations that can take your life off course.

    B. Consistent living is not a one-time event, but a daily journey.

    C. Consistent living will enable you to reach your goals more quickly.

1. How can you become more consistent in working toward your purpose?

_____

_____

_____

_____

2. How has a lack of consistency kept you from living your purpose?

_____

_____

_____

_____

3. How can you maintain balance in life and stay consistent in living your purpose?

_____

_____

_____

_____

"We are what we repeatedly do. Excellence, therefore, is not an act but a habit." Aristotle

5. Confidence

"Then they said to him, "We have had a dream and there is no one to interpret it." Then Joseph said to them, "Do not interpretations belong to God? Tell it to me, please." Genesis 40:8

Confidence is the assurance and reliance in the abilities and gifts that God has entrusted you with to accomplish His purpose.

A. Your confidence is often the only difference between success and failure

B. Your confidence determines how you approach life.

C. Your confidence is the foundation for turning problems into potential solutions.

1. Give an example of a time you had to show confidence after being rejected?

_____

_____

_____

_____

2. Have you ever become too confident in your own abilities rather than trusting in God? What was the outcome?

_____

_____

_____

_____

3. In what areas of life do you need to be confident in the abilities that God has given you?

_____

_____

_____

_____

4. Reflect on a time when you were very confident that you were moving in the right direction and it seemed things were going well; then a tragedy, distraction or disappointment occurred and totally knocked you off course. How did you respond? Were you able to overcome the tragedy, distraction or disappointment? What can you do if something similar happens again?

_____

_____

_____

_____

_____

_____

"Nobody can make you feel inferior without your consent." Eleanor Roosevelt

6. Courage

"I had a dream last night, Pharaoh told him, and none of these men can tell me what it means. But I have heard that you can interpret dreams, and that is why I have called for you. It is beyond my power to do this, Joseph replied. But God will tell you what it means and will set you at ease."
Genesis 41:15-16

Courage is standing when everyone else wants to run, speaking when everyone is afraid to speak, acting when everyone is paralyzed by fear, taking action in the face of danger, holding one's character and moral uprightness when everyone else is tempted to compromise theirs.

    A. A lack of courage gives the enemy the fuel he needs to take over your territory.

    B. Courage empowers you to do what you are afraid of doing.

    C. "For God has not given us a spirit of fear, but of power, love and a sound mind." I Timothy 1:7

1. What area in your life have you had to display courage in overcoming an obstacle or challenge? How did you overcome the obstacle or challenge or what do you need to do to overcome the obstacle or challenge?

_____

_____

_____

_____

_____

2. How will you display courage and live your purpose even in the face of fear?

_____

_____

_____

_____

_____

3. How have you shown courage in a difficult time? Explain.

_____

_____

_____

_____

_____

"Courage is the mastery of fear, not the absence of fear." Mark Twain

7. Communicate

"Now let Pharaoh look for a man discerning and wise, and set him over the land of Egypt. Let Pharaoh take action to appoint overseers in charge of the land and let him exact a fifth of the product of the land of Egypt in the seven years of abundance." Genesis 41:33-34

Communication is the outward expression of your purpose to the world through verbal and nonverbal actions.

A. You must find a way to effectively communicate your purpose to the world.

B. Effective communication has more to do with listening than with talking.

C. Your actions must speak louder than the words you say.

1. In what ways can you effectively communicate your purpose?

_____

_____

_____

_____

_____

2. How are you going to communicate your purpose on a daily basis?

_____

_____

_____

_____

_____

3. Have you discussed your purpose with your spouse, close friend or a trusted family member? What was their response? How can they help you in your pursuit of purpose?

_____

_____

_____

_____

_____

"Think twice before you speak, because your words and influence will plant the seed of either success or failure in the mind of another." Napoleon Hill

Seven Poisons to Purpose

1. **Desperation** – You do things contrary to the character God wants you to display.
2. **Defeat** – You feel like a failure so you do not pursue your purpose.
3. **Diversions** – You become more attracted to the wrong things than the right things.
4. **Doubt** - You question God's purpose for your life.
5. **Delays** – You put off doing what you know you need to do.
6. **Discouragement** - You focus on your problems rather than possible solutions.
7. **Disclaimers** – You talk against the purpose God desires for your life.

1. What poisons have you allowed to distract you from living out your purpose? How can you overcome these poisonous distractions?

_____

_____

_____

_____

_____

_____

_____

_____

2. Reflection: As you go through your daily walk in life, thank God for His direction and gracious benefits: your salvation, health, job, salary, family, food, transportation, shelter, church, spouse and so forth. Giving thanks in all things forces you to remember that God is in control. Take some time to write a prayer of thanksgiving and petition for His directions from your heart that you can pray on a daily basis.

_____

_____

_____

_____

_____

_____

_____

_____

"Do not go where the path may lead instead go where there is no path and leave a trail."
Ralph Waldo Emerson

Chapter 3
Define Your Values
Daniel 3

Define Your Values

"If it be so, our God whom we serve is able to deliver us from the burning fiery furnace, and he will deliver us out of thine hand, O king. But, if not, be it known unto thee, O king, that we will not serve thy gods, nor worship the golden image which thou hast set up." Daniel 3: 17-18

Do you have prioritized core values that direct your daily life? Are you so connected with living your core values that you would give up an opportunity that was not ethical even though no one else would know? Are you willing to walk away from a few moments of pleasure and stand firm on what you believe is right to do?

The three Hebrew boys (Shadrach, Meshach and Abednego) are great examples of what it means to live your core values. Even under extreme pressure from the king to worship his idol god, living their core values was non-negotiable.

What are Values?

Values are deeply held beliefs that define what is right and fundamentally important to each of us. They provide guidelines for your daily choices and actions.

The Hebrew boys were so committed to living their core values that when the king threatened to throw them in the fiery furnace because they would not bow to his idol, they did not give in. They did not know whether they would be delivered from the fiery furnace or not, but without wavering they did not back down on what they valued.

Your core values should be:

- *Clearly Stated*
- *Conscientiously Chosen*
- *Continually Executed*
- *Consistently Followed*
- *Constantly Evaluated*

To become effective in your life's journey you need to identify and develop clear and concise core values. Your core values are central to defining who you are, what you do and where you are going. Once defined, they should guide you in every aspect of your life. When you make a conscious decision to follow your core values you will not let anyone or anything persuade you to live against them. It is these core values that determine what is important to you as an individual.

The surprising thing is that, if you ask most people what their core values are, many could not give you a solid answer. Some would give you a list of values, but they would not be able to prioritize them. They will give you a list that sounds spiritual, but they don't come close to living them. I believe in order to live the vision that God has designed for you effectively; you must have a set of prioritized core values that guides your daily life.

Take some time to answer the following questions to help develop your prioritized core values. I advise you to seek God to establish your core values. Once you establish your core values and start living them, watch your life begin to turn in a different and more positive direction. Do not get frustrated and quit if it at first it seems difficult living your core values, but keep praying and moving through the process.

Personal Application Questions:

1. What values have been present in your life since childhood?

_____

_____

_____

_____

_____

_____

_____

2. List 5 to 7 important values in your life? Prioritize these values.

_____

_____

_____

_____

_____

_____

_____

3. What do these values really mean to you?

_____

_____

_____

_____

_____

_____

_____

4. How do you expect to live the core values you defined?

_____

_____

_____

_____

_____

_____

_____

5. Would you give up a job, friends, monetary gain, prestige and power to live your values? Why would you give up any of these things? Why might it be hard to give up any of these things?

_____

_____

_____

_____

_____

_____

_____

6. Do your core values line up with God's values? If not, what changes do you need to implement in your life to make sure your values are in line with God's values?

_____

_____

_____

_____

_____

> ### What Does God Value?
>
> *"But the fruit of the Spirit is love, joy, peace, patience, kindness, goodness, faithfulness, gentleness, self-control; against such things there is no law." Galatians 5: 22-23*

_____

_____

_____

_____

_____

_____

7. Why do you believe it is important for you to have prioritized values that you live by daily?

_____

_____

_____

_____

_____

_____

_____

_____

_____

_____

"Many people die with their music still in them. Why is this so? Too often it is because they are always getting ready to live. Before they know it, time runs out." Oliver Wendell Holmes

Focus Forward

"Brethren, I do not regard myself as having laid hold of it yet; but one thing I do: forgetting what lies behind and reaching forward to what lies ahead. I press on toward the goal for the prize of the upward call of God in Christ Jesus." Philippians 3:13-14

What past events in your life have caused you to lose focus? How can you focus forward in your vision when life presents overwhelming circumstances? To achieve the success God has for you, you must first focus on your definite purpose. A definite purpose is your life's overall direction. What do you see for your life? Is it a successful marriage, a loving family, your own unique business? Is it the ownership of property or personal assets? Whatever your vision is, you can only accomplish it by focus.

Paul likens himself to a person running a race to receive the winning prize. The runner lines up in the starting blocks along with the other

> *"Always focus on the front windshield and not the review mirror." Colin Powell*

runners in the race. He hears the starting gun go off and he begins to run the race. As the runner takes off, his eyes are focused on the finish line. His eyes are not focused on the runners on either side of him. He is focused straight ahead. He understands if he takes his eyes off the prize and focuses on the other runners he will be in danger of losing the race.

His ultimate goal is to cross the finish line ahead of the other runners to win the prize. The prize is what motivates the runner to run the race. Whatever God has purposed for your life is possible to achieve, but you must run your race and focus on your prize. Your race is for you to run and no one can run it for you.

The prize that a runner receives for winning a race is an earthly prize that soon fades with the passing of time. The prize I am referring to is not some deteriorating earthly reward, but it encompasses all that you will receive in this life and the life to come. It takes more than just working hard at something. You must know what to work hard at in order to accomplish your purpose, live your values, see your future, set your goals and work your plan.

If you have too many pursuits, you can become easily sidetracked. Successful people know that one of the key factors to achieving success is that you must visualize and focus on the prize that is set before you. Focus sets your mentality to aim straight for a goal, while blocking out other unproductive thoughts and distractions from your mind. Your abilities and gifts are more honed and tuned in when you are focused.

Personal Application Questions:

1. What past failures can you use to help shape where you are going?

_____

_____

_____

_____

2. What past failures have kept you from moving forward in your vision?

_____

_____

_____

_____

3. How can you overcome your past failures and live forward?

_____

_____

_____

_____

4. What past successes can you use as motivation in moving your vision forward?

_____

_____

_____

_____

5. What past successes have led you to live a comfortable and complacent life? What do you need to do to move from your comfortable and complacent life to where God wants you to be?

_____

_____

_____

_____

_____

"Many of life's failures are people who did not realize how close they were to success when they gave up." Thomas Edison

Chapter 4
See Your Future
Genesis 12

See Your Future

"Now the Lord said to Abram Go forth from your country, and from your relatives and from your father's house, to the land which I will show you." Genesis 12:1

God has designed an incredible future for you. He desires for you to have a successful vision that will impact the future of every area of your life. When God begins to unfold your vision for your future, you will need to have the faith to walk it out daily. Your life progress depends on it. Your family is relying on it. Individuals you do not know will be blessed by it.

You must see the promise of your future even though your present situation is totally opposite of where you need and desire to be. You may ask, "How

> **Picture of the Future**
>
> *Is a clear picture of where you believe God is directing your life. Your future focuses on where you are going and not where you have been and on the end results and not the process for getting there.*

can I accomplish this?" You accomplish it by keeping your focus on your promised future and blocking out all of the unnecessary distractions.

Open your ears, mind and heart to the sound of your vision. It may be a faint sound smothered by life's circumstances, but it's still playing. Your past mistakes may try to resurface to drown out your future progress, but the beat of your vision can still be heard in the background.

People may tell you what you can and what you should do, but you tell them you are following the sound of your vision. You must have faith that the future God promised you will come to pass in spite of everything happening around you. You can start today by taking the necessary steps to prepare you and your family for your promised future.

When you look at your future through the lens of God's Word, the impossible becomes possible. The unreachable becomes reachable. The conquered becomes the conqueror. See your future and live as God sees and watch your vision come to pass.

"I have a dream that one day on the red hills of Georgia the sons of former slaves and the sons of former slave owners will be able to sit down together at the table of brotherhood... I have a dream." Martin Luther King Jr. "I have a dream"

Your Dream List

"Delight yourself in the Lord; and He will give you the desires of your heart. Commit your way to the Lord, trust also in Him, and He will do it." Psalms 37:4-5

Create your dream list. List some things you want to do, places you want to go, things you want to own and goals you want to achieve. This is your dream list! Do not be reserved and do not look at your current situation. Date each dream when you enter it and indicate one of the seven areas of life it pertains to (Spiritual, Physical, Mental, Financial, Relational, Social and Professional). Have fun!

Date	Dream	Area of Life

Date	Dream	Area of Life

Date	Dream	Area of Life

Date	Dream	Area of Life

Can you begin to see your future? Write your future (vision) in detail for the seven areas of your life. Refer to your dream list and answers to questions that you have written in the workbook. Listen to God's direction for each area of your life.

7 Areas of Life to Focus your Future:

1. Spiritual – (relationship with God, prayer, Bible study, faith, worship, church)
2. Physical – (medical health, exercise, appearance, weight, nutrition, dental, vision)
3. Relational – (spouse, children, family, friends, forgiveness, love, honor, respect)
4. Mental – (education, reading, listening, creativity, imagination, thoughts, attitude)
5. Professional – (vocation, job, training, co-workers, employees, career, resume)
6. Social – (activities, people, events, habits, dates, family outings, vacations)
7. Financial – (earnings, savings, investments, giving, debt, spending, budgets)

Spiritual:_____

_____

_____

_____

Relational:_____

_____

_____

_____

Physical:_____

_____

_____

_____

Mental:_____
        .
_____
_____
_____

Social:_____
_____
_____
_____

Financial:_____
_____
_____
_____

Professional:_____
_____
_____
_____

"Take the first step in faith. You don't have to see the whole staircase, just take the first step."
Dr. Martin Luther King, Jr.

Chapter 5
Set Your Goals
Nehemiah 1-7

Set Your Goals

"Then I said to them, 'You see the bad situation we are in, that Jerusalem is desolate and its gates burned by fire. Come; let us rebuild the wall of Jerusalem so that we will no longer be a reproach." Nehemiah 2: 17

Goal setting is an extremely powerful tool for accomplishing your life's vision. If you ask most people what their goals and plans for their life or families are, many would not be able to give you specifics. Some would give vague and unrealistic answers and say things like, "I want to be wealthy," or "do God's will," or "own a business." They will give general answers that are not goals but rather dreams desired by many people.

What is a Goal?

A goal is an aim, a purpose or a sense of direction toward which you move all of your energies, desires and efforts. Goals are the targets toward which you point your life. A goal involves an organized, planned stretching of your life.

Goals are not written in concrete or unchangeable terms, but they do give you a starting point and a destination to reach. I am not promising a magical formula that guarantees that your goals will automatically happen if you read this material or attend some expert's seminar. Nor am I suggesting that if you follow our twelve steps you will have no struggles and everything will happen in your life the way you want at the exact time you desire.

Once you have a goals plan - now what? Many people agree on the positive impact that a goal-setting plan can have. Many individuals have used goal-planning sheets to list their major goals, but that is where they stopped. They defined their goals, but never implemented the plan.

Do something each and every day toward the accomplishment of your goals. Work with passion and energy on the first step of your plan until it is either completed or until you can make no further progress on it. Then move to the next step, coming back to those incomplete steps as soon as you can move them forward to their completion. Keep moving! Keep working! Keep taking action steps every day! Do not stop! Your life has greater meaning when you are working toward the goals you desire.

List 5 Goals that you want to accomplish:

1._____

_____

_____

_____

_____

_____

| **12 simple steps to achieving your goals:** |
| 1. *Seek God for your goals.* |
| 2. *Define your goals in writing.* |
| 3. *Create measures to success.* |
| 4. *Define possible opportunities for success.* |
| 5. *Identify barriers to success.* |
| 6. *Break down goals into strategic action steps.* |
| 7. *Identify resources, skills and/or people needed* |
| 8. *Develop new habits.* |
| 9. *Take consistent action.* |
| 10. *Monitor your goals regularly.* |
| 11. *Reward yourself.* |
| 12. *Keep moving forward.* |

2._____

_____

_____

_____

_____

3._____

_____

_____

4._____

_____

_____

5._____

_____

_____

From the five goals that you listed, choose two of them and work through our 12 Simple Steps to Achieving Your Goals. We have included three Goals Matter! Planning Sheets for you to write your goals, and an example of a written goal to help guide you through the process. The example is a goal of someone desiring to become debt free by July 15, 2018.

"A dream is just a dream. A goal is a dream with a plan and a deadline." Harvey Mackay

Example: Goals Matter! Planning Sheet

Goal: (specific, measurable, actionable, reinforcing and trackable)
I am debt free by 9/15/2019.

Measures to success:

Term of Goal: _____ Short-Term (within 1 year) **X** Med.-Term (within 3 years)
_____Long-Term (Over 3 Years)

Life Area (circle one): Spiritual– Relational – Physical– Social - ***Financial***– Mental - Professional
Begin Date: _____**1/10/16**_____Target Completion Date: _____**9/15/19**_____
Actual Completion Date:_____

Possible opportunities for success: (What will you get from accomplishing this goal?)		
1. Less Stress	4. Remodel home	7. Give more
2. Pay house off early	5. Financial freedom	
3. Buy new wardrobe	6. Travel	

Barriers to success: (Things that can prohibit you from achieving this goal.)
1. Impulse spending
2. Unexpected expenses (Hospital bills, car problems, appliances breakdown)
3. Not enough money coming in
4. Job loss/ pay cut

New habit(s): (What new daily habits can you implement to make this goal a reality?)
1. Implement a plan to monitor daily, weekly and monthly spending.
2. Take lunch to work at least 4x a week and cook on weekend.

Strategic Action Steps for Achieving this Goal	Begin date	Target Date	Completed date
1. Pay off $4,000 doctor bill	1/10/16	9/10/16	11/15/16
2. Pay off $5,000 furniture bill	1/10/16	12/15/16	1/30/17
3. Pay off $7,500 Tax bill	3/10/16	5/10/17	11/15/16
4. Pay off $13,500 Student loan	3/20/16	12/31/18	
5. Pay off $17,000 Credit Card	4/10/16	9/15/19	
6.			
7.			
8.			
9.			
10.			

What resources, skills and/or people do I need to accomplish this goal?
1. A solid spending plan
2. Spouse and children support
3. A goal monitoring system
4. A Financial Analysis
5. An accountability partner

Affirmations to support this goal:
1. I am debt free by 9/15/2019
2. I am not a slave to the lender
3. I will stay on target despite any obstacles or difficulties
4. I will overcome any urges to sidetrack from our plan of becoming debt free

Is this goal worth the time, effort or money required? (Circle)	Yes		No
Does this goal support my values? (Circle)	Yes		No

Goals Matter! Planning Sheet

Goal: (specific, measurable, actionable, reinforcing and trackable)

Measures to success:

Term of Goal: ___ Short-Term (within 1 year) ___ Med.-Term (within 3 years)
_____ Long-Term (Over 3 Years)

Life Area (circle one): Spiritual– Relational – Physical– Social - Financial– Mental - Professional
Begin Date: _____ Target Completion Date: _____
Actual Completion Date: _____

Possible opportunities for success: (What will you get from accomplishing this goal?)

Barriers to success: (Things that can prohibit you from achieving this goal.)

New habit(s): (What new daily habits can you implement to make this goal a reality?)

Strategic Action Steps for Achieving this Goal	Begin date	Target Date	Completed date

What resources, skills and/or people do I need to accomplish this goal?

Affirmations to support this goal:

Is this goal worth the time, effort or money required? (Circle)	Yes	No
Does this goal support my values? (Circle)	Yes	No

Goals Matter! Planning Sheet

Goal: (specific, measurable, actionable, reinforcing and trackable)

| |
| |
| |

Measures to success:

Term of Goal: ___ Short-Term (within 1 year) ___Med.-Term (within 3 years) _____Long-Term (Over 3 Years)

Life Area (circle one): Spiritual– Relational – Physical– Social - Financial– Mental - Professional

Begin Date: _____Target Completion Date: _____

Actual Completion Date:_____

Possible opportunities for success: (What will you get from accomplishing this goal?)

| |
| |
| |

Barriers to success: (Things that can prohibit you from achieving this goal.)

| |
| |
| |
| |

New habit(s): (What new daily habits can you implement to make this goal a reality?)

| |
| |
| |

Strategic Action Steps for Achieving this Goal	Begin date	Target Date	Completed date

What resources, skills and/or people do I need to accomplish this goal?

Affirmations to support this goal:

Is this goal worth the time, effort or money required? (Circle)	Yes	No
Does this goal support my values? (Circle)	Yes	No

Goals Matter! Planning Sheet

Goal: (specific, measurable, actionable, reinforcing and trackable)

Measures to success:

Term of Goal: ____ Short-Term (within 1 year) ___Med.-Term (within 3 years) _____Long-Term (Over 3 Years)

Life Area (circle one): Spiritual– Relational – Physical– Social - Financial– Mental - Professional

Begin Date: _____Target Completion Date: _____

Actual Completion Date:_____

Possible opportunities for success: (What will you get from accomplishing this goal?)

Barriers to success: (Things that can prohibit you from achieving this goal.)

New habit(s): (What new daily habits can you implement to make this goal a reality?)

Strategic Action Steps for Achieving this Goal	Begin date	Target Date	Completed date

What resources, skills and/or people do I need to accomplish this goal?

Affirmations to support this goal:

Is this goal worth the time, effort or money required? (Circle)	Yes	No
Does this goal support my values? (Circle)	Yes	No

73

Chapter 6
Work Your Plan
James 1: 21-25

Work Your Plan

"But prove yourselves doers of the Word, and not merely hearers who delude themselves."
James 1:22

Now that you have written your purpose statement, listed your core values, set your goals and described your future, it is time to work your vision plan. It is great to have a well-written plan that you and others can see and reference, but it does you no good to have a well-written plan if you do not work it.

The plan God gives you is the plan He desires for you to activate. You cannot afford to sit back and wait and think that God is going to hand you a free ride to living your vision. You must go to work.

In working your vision plan, you will encounter challenges and obstacles that will try to make you quit. They will come at you daily with negative thoughts and words of failure, but you must remain focused on your plan. Paul said it best: "I press on toward the goal for the prize of the upward call of God in Christ Jesus" (Philippians 3:14).

> *"The price of success is hard work, dedication to the job at hand and the determination that whether we win or lose, we have applied the best of ourselves to the task at hand." Vince Lombardi*

Paul had a vision plan to get to his ultimate goal and he wasn't going to let anyone or anything stop him. He pressed forward. When people tell you it is not going to happen, you have to keep pressing. When you tell yourself you are not going to make it, you have to keep pushing forward. When you are tired and defeat looks imminent, you must keep fighting.

You must tirelessly stand against the temptations that will try to settle you into a comfort zone. You must fight to overcome the intense desire to procrastinate. You cannot afford to let laziness and slothfulness infiltrate your life. You have a vision to work.

The enemy wants to keep you complacent, fearful and doubtful. He does not want you to even try to live your vision. He will give you a good job; a wonderful position, a large salary, a nice bank account and prized possessions that will make you feel important. They masquerade as the real thing, but in reality, they can become the very things that keep you from living your intended vision. You must remind yourself over and over, day after day that if you keep working God's plan, then your vision can become a reality.

You can start today living your life the way God designed by working your vision plan. Here is our simple process we discovered and implemented for working your vision plan. Please view each process with an open mind and answer the questions honestly with a simple yes or no. If you answer more no's than yes's, you have some work to do.

A. Personal Responsibility

- Realize Your Vision – Are you in position to realize your vision from God?
- Write Your Vision – Do you have a written vision plan for your life and/or family?
- Post Your Vision – Have you posted your vision so those who are connected to it can see it?
- Work Your Vision – Are you prepared to work toward your vision at all cost?
- Wait for Your Vision – Are you willing to wait patiently for your vision to happen?

B. Vision Realization

- Purposeful – Does your vision have a definite purpose?
- Passion – Do you have passion to see your vision fulfilled?
- Progressive – Are you ready to progress forward in living your vision?
- Protect – Are you willing to protect your vision at all cost?
- Patient – Can you wait on your vision without getting in the way?
- Profitable – Is your vision profitable to those that are connected to you?
- Powerful – Do you have a powerful vision that will outlive you?

C. Discipline Management

- Alone Time – Do you have a quiet uninterruptable time alone for personal reflection, meditation and prayer?

- Stewardship – Are you a good steward of the resources God has given you?

- Work Ethics – Have you developed solid work ethics as you move toward your vision?

- Personal Development – Are you developing daily to become the person God has designed you to be?

- Servant Leadership –Does your vision serve others or is it only self-serving?

D. Continual Improvement

- Vision Review – Do you review your vision periodically to see where you are?

- Goals Review – Do you review your written goals to ensure that you are on track?

- Self-Examination – Do you perform a daily self-examination of your internal and external life?

- Living Values – Do you have prioritized core values that you are committed to living daily?

- Corrective and Preventive Action – Are there actions in your life you need to correct or prevent?

"It is good to dream, but it is better to dream and work. Faith is mighty, but action with faith is mightier. Desiring is helpful, but work and desire are invincible." Thomas Robert Gaines

The World is Waiting for Your Vision

"Now unto Him who is able to do exceeding, abundantly and above all that we ask or think, according to the power that works within us." Ephesians 3:20

The world is waiting for you to make an impact with your vision. You cannot wait for the perfect timing; the right situation or the right economic climate. You must start pursuing your vision now.

It is up to you to decide whether you will live the life God designed for you. God has done all He is going to do; now the rest is up to you. He is expecting you to make your move. He is waiting for you to step up to the plate.

> *"Friends time waits for no one. It moves on and keeps moving on. It does not stop for anything or anybody. It doesn't matter how much money you have, how much power you have, or how much prestige you have – time keeps moving on. Everybody has the same amount of time twenty-four hours per day not one minute more." Willie Jolley*

You don't have to attend another seminar or workshop, watch another program or listen to another vision sermon to move your vision forward. It is time to do what you know to do. Every day you do not implement your vision is another day that you and the world miss your contribution.

Whatever God is calling you to, I admonish you to walk in it. Do not let anyone, including your family, the enemy, others or even yourself, talk you out of your promise. You do not know what God will do with the book you write, the job you apply for, the business you start or the person you share the Gospel with.

If you do things God's way and not the world's way, you could be walking into a top selling book, a multi-million dollar business or sharing the Gospel that changes someone's eternal destiny.

You do not know what God can do through you until you do what He designed you to do. I am not promising that you'll be a millionaire, everyone will love you or that everything will happen the way you want, but I know when you realize your purpose from God, your life will never be the same.

Colors will become brighter, words will become more powerful, time will not be wasted, your energy will rise and your vision will become clearer. Start living your vision today because the world is waiting for what's in you.

"... I refuse to rummage through my trash heap of failures. I will admit them. I will correct them. I will press on. Victoriously. No failure is fatal. It's OK to stumble...I will get up. It's OK to fail...I will rise again. Today I will make a difference."   Max Lucado

Appendix A – Form to write your vision statement

Write Your Vision

"And the Lord answered me, and said 'Write the vision and make it plain upon tables, that he may run that reads it." Habakkuk 2:2

Now is the time to write a vision statement for your life. God will give you a vision that will raise a thirst and hunger in you like never before. You may not totally understand everything that God reveals to you, but write it down anyway.

What you write down may not match your current situation. What you write down may seem unachievable. What you write down may look crazy to others and even you. But if God said it, you can take it to the bank and cash it. He may give you a plan to pay off your debt even though you are broke. He may give you a plan for a business even if you do not have the experience. He may give you a plan for a successful marriage even if you are still single. Whatever He reveals to you, write it down and start moving toward it.

Your written vision statement is your plan to put into action. Once you write it down the way you like,

> *"Every man is born into the world to do something unique and something distinctive and if he does not do it, it will never be done." Benjamin E. Mays*

type it on one page and frame it. Just as a business or organization posts its vision statement, I encourage you to post your framed vision statement in a visible location in your home so that you are reminded daily of God's specific vision for your life and/or family.

Please review what you have written in your workbook for knowing your purpose, living your values and seeing your future. On the following form, draft your personal or family vision statement. Once you have a written vision statement you are happy with, frame it and begin to live it.

"Where there is no vision the people perish…." Proverbs 29:18

Write your purpose statement. (See the section "Know Your Purpose" in the workbook)

Write your values in prioritize order. (See the section "Live Your Values" in the workbook)

How do you see your Future? (Spiritual, Relational, Physical, Mental, Social, Financial, Professional)   (See the section "See Your Future" in the workbook)

Brandon Doe
Personal Vision Statement

Purpose:

I help bring out the color within people's lives by encouraging, equipping and empowering them to live the life God designed them to live.

My Core Values:

1. Growing Relationship with God
2. Becoming One Flesh with My Wife.
3. Training our Children God's Way.
4. Encouraging Family and Friends
5. Excellent Physical Health
6. Daily Peace of Mind
7. Financial Freedom
8. Continual Personal Development

Seeing My Future (Vision):

- I have a daily loving relationship with God that places Christ at the center of my life, the Word of God as my manual for living and the Holy Spirit as my director.

- I love, honor and respect my wife so we become one flesh daily in our marriage.

- I am a Godly father and role model for my sons so they have a blueprint for how to become an effective and productive man.

- I encourage and bless my family, friends and those individuals God connects me with.

- I own and lead a successful $2 million+ business that help people live their vision.

- I make wise investments and spending decisions that allow us to live debt free, leave a financial generation inheritance, bless others and live the lifestyle of our choice.

- I live a healthy lifestyle that keeps my mind at peace, gives me energy to do God's will, maintains my ideal body weight, allows me to participate in recreational activities and live disease free.

When my life is over, I want to hear God say "You finished your course and kept the faith; you fulfilled My vision for your life and now it is time to enter into My eternal rest."

Christ the Center

"That if you confess with your mouth Jesus as Lord, and believe in your heart that God raised Him from the dead, you will be saved; for with the heart a person believes, resulting in righteousness, and with the mouth he confesses, resulting in salvation." Romans 10: 9-10

As we have discussed in this workbook God created every person with a unique vision. He knew from the very beginning of time who He designed you to be and what He destined you to do. You were created with a specific purpose and clear vision in mind. The only way you can truly fulfill your purpose and live your vision is for Christ to be the center of your life.

The only way for Christ to be the center of your life is for you to accept Him as your Savior and Lord and obey His directions. Your mother, father, grandmother, friend,

> *"When Christ is the center of your life you can then truly live the purpose that you were created to live and accomplish the vision He designed for your life."*

mentor nor your pastor can accept Christ on your behalf. You have to make a willful decision to put your trust in Him.

When you accept Christ as Savior and Lord and allow Him to become the center of your life, you will begin to develop an overwhelming desire to become the person He designed you to be. When you accept Christ in your life, He becomes committed to seeing His vision for your life come to pass.

"....I am come that you might have life and have life more abundantly." John 10:10

Christ stands waiting for you to accept Him. He desires to be the center of your life. He wants to give you the desires of your heart as you delight in Him. When you set aside your own personal aims, goals and ambitions and choose His desires, He will open up your vision in incredible ways.

Christ wants to take you to where only He can keep you. The vision He has for you will overflow in every area of your life. He stands ready to help you succeed beyond your greatest dreams.

Have you accepted Christ as your Lord and Savior? If not, it is time to humble yourself and surrender to Him because you will never be all the man you can be unless you have a personal relationship with Christ. It is time to give Him your heart so you can live your vision with power. Please pray the following prayer with a humble heart to receive God's salvation.

Dear Lord,

I know that I am a sinner and I need Your forgiveness. I can no longer live the way that I have been living. I need a Savior in my life. I believe that Christ died for my sins on the cross and that God raised Him from the grave on the third day with all power. I want to turn from my sins and turn to Christ. I now invite Him to come into my heart. I want to trust and follow Him as my Savior and Lord. I want to realize my vision and live it out the way He designed for my life. I will now use my life to glorify Him. In Jesus name. Amen.

If you have a personal relationship with Christ, but you are not in total alignment with His vision for your life, now is the time to let Him do the driving. Pray this prayer to get your life in line with His vision.

Heavenly Father,

I come to you because I need You to align my life to the vision you designed for me to live. I admit that I have tried to live my vision in my way. I ask You to forgive me for not following your vision for my life. I want You to direct my life's vision from this moment forward. I want to be the man You designed me to be. I want to be the visionary for my life and family. I surrender fully to Your vision for every area of my life. And whenever I get off course, I know that I can come to You to get back on course. I thank you for hearing my prayer and aligning my life to your vision. In Jesus name. Amen.

"I am the vine, you are the branches; he who abides in Me and I in him, he bears much fruit, for apart from Me you can do nothing." John 15:5

Notes

Notes

www.ingramcontent.com/pod-product-compliance
Lightning Source LLC
Chambersburg PA
CBHW062051090426
42740CB00016B/3100